SUNLIGHT
LATER

Sunlight Later
© Jo Matthews / Cathexis Northwest Press

No part of this book may be reproduced without written permission
of the publisher or author, except in reviews and articles.

First Printing: 2025

ISBN: 978-1-952869-97-6

Cover Photo by Janis Wolf
Editing & Design by C. M. Tollefson
Cathexis Northwest Press

cathexisnorthwestpress.com

SUNLIGHT
LATER

Poems by
Jo Matthews

Cathexis Northwest Press

For Koji

Table of Contents

What things to notice	1
A selection of things that have made it onto my long-term memory: Part 2	3
Pink Moon	4
At the corner of Hoofdweg	5
Day Off	7
Lonely	9
Last night we heard a shooting	10
A walk in the park	11
Lullaby	13
Breathe	15
When I wake to feed my daughter	16
Sometimes, who I am	18
Light on the water	19
Vespers	20
A selection of things that have made it onto my long-term memory: Part 1	22
Anything could happen	24
These Days	26
Post Traumatic Silence	27
A butterfly landed in my palm	29
Message from Earthside	30
Fetching Isla	31
Second Marriage	33

If I was going to die tomorrow	34
Things I nearly didn't notice on a day I felt depressed	35
Watching Dumbo in Yokohama	36
And what about the prayers?	38
Note-to-self	40
There are many ways to view a body	41
Birds	42
A selection of things that have made it onto my long-term memory: Part 3	43
Dream	44

'There will be time to audit
The accounts later, there will be sunlight later
And the equation will come out at last.'

Louis MacNeice

Autumn Journal, Part XXIV

What things to notice

It's too late again
I meant to go to bed an hour ago

rub pointless potions quickly, haphazardly
into the folds of my face, screw up my eyes for concertina lines
that stay put like pencil outlines before

the ink black overlay, pull my cheeks up to my ears
then watch them sink back all the way

wonder if I should give up sugar
or invest in some other expensive cream

but learn to rub it in right, like how they show you
massaging myself like a queen, like how I'm meant to

but only if I can get to bed earlier
- why can't I get to bed earlier?

and I wonder if these things are

    the things to notice

or if I will get to the end and realise all the things

    I could have noticed instead

like I could notice the way
the clouds swell up solidly like sacred kingdoms
or how the sky fades black to morning white to hide the stars

or I could notice water curling over rocks like shining muscle
or shadows dancing to silence on whitewashed walls

    or I could notice the way it might all be over in a day

like at the corner of my street where the traffic lights

are bound with flowers
sunflowers roses carnations lilies
spilling onto the street in black buckets circled by red candle holders

she was 31 and the truck didn't see
her bike as she rode across the road

and I wonder what she was noticing just then:
was it her lines and her mess and her unanswered texts

    or was it the way the wind kissed her face?

I could notice the way the wind kissed my face

or I could notice
sheet rain willow snapping gold leaves
or great lungfuls of birds freewheeling across winter skies

or I could notice the way the two people I prayed most to come
did come - they are in the next room sleeping

notice my veins like old rivers
sending life to my heart, still beating

still breathing, in still unnoticed glory

notice the lines on my face

    that tell only my story.

A selection of things that have made it onto my long-term memory: Part 2

this thought: I'd better love him if he says he loves me

a fairy story starts at Everest Base Camp – a fitting peak – and
of course, I said yes, yes like a princess in a puffed white

dress, hearing the click-click of the photographer and knowing
my hair will look *perfect* in that photo, all plaited and honeyed

and new and later, him chasing me home, him throwing his
phone (at the wall or at me, I wasn't sure) and later

him telling me I was like Marmite: you either loved me or
you hated me and this thought: that is a strange thing to say to

your wife, him insisting I watch him sign the divorce papers
– but slowly – then seeing him for the last time under the glare

of a tangerine streetlight, light falling like a Hollywood movie
moon, then wanting to feel new and buying towels, pink ones,

an outrageously-floral bedspread, a mediumly-expensive
gold-plated ring, and chrysanthemums and cigarettes from

Tesco's, the taste of white wine and white dust at the back
of my throat, walking home at 8am, crying at the mothers

with their babies and the joggers and the couples with their
coffees but, oh kind world! there is always some *thing*

to ease the pain, an easy exchange for stuff or substance
to fill me up, the desperate dehydrated howl of waking up

naked and uncovered and alone and without my phone
and knowing I hadn't said yes but wondering if I'd said no

and later, Amsterdam and one suitcase, just to breathe in
and out of old orbits of abuse, canals sinking new shame

into the watery memories of earth.

Pink Moon

If the clouds are accommodating
then tonight's full "pink moon" will be a little bit bigger in the sky

as our planet's only satellite is almost as close to us as its orbit allows.
But beware the misconceptions about the names people give to moons:

"The pink moon is named not because it will take on a particular colour
But because of the colour of the flowering phlox, coming into bloom"

say the astrophysicists. So no, the moon definitely won't be pink
"unless there is pollution in the air and it could take on a reddish tinge"

and anyway, will it be worth the early start? The moon is the same moon
wherever you are, but do I want it to superimpose its spurious pinkness

here   onto my memory of the last time I saw it so big   there

back when my hands were small and worries were smaller
eye pressed tight to Dad's big red telescope angled towards home

skies and familiar constellations, me in my pink pyjamas and
the too-big communal coat that smelled of bonfires and apples

just turned, the other eye squeezed shut to let the moonlight
flood the finder, its dark orange light leaking through

the lens to mine, craters too real to be real, shadows bleeding
to dark, our planet's only satellite open-mouthed in sorrow's song.

And I wondered if it was really sad, or maybe just thinking,
if it was really alone, or maybe just waiting.

At the corner of Hoofdweg

seagulls fly in packs
hunters of concrete kingdoms
gliding winter gusts

these scaremongers of pigeons
these denizens of dirty

they scour chicken bones,
peanut shells, they soar air-high
arcs, paint flashed silver

shadows onto windowpanes
as clouds of old masters still

roll above. a tram
sighs by. people board in masks,
people sleep in small

windowed boxed, people walk
in unmapped constellations

people wait for next
and better and when, and for
days to start and end.

around the corner, under
the water, a terrapin

wonders if it's time
to wake, raindrops hang silent
on leaves, black branches

shake sleep, readying for spring –
which will come as it always

does – and easily.
ducks groom emerald-slicked wings
heron folds neck back

into its jurassic home
snowdrops crack steel-shining spines

in tenacity
against the dimming day. roots
wait, humming their plans

to old earth; their forgotten
music; their mud-buried light.

Day Off

silver parcels stack like tiny sandwiches
    on my head, a masked face stares back from
        the mirror. I'm thankful it's masked, that way I can

only be critical from the nose up. 'There!'
    says the hairdresser, finishing with a fluster
        of hairspray and a twizzle of the chair. I wonder why

I still waste my time with this shit, but it's because
    I still hope I will look, can look, *honeyed* and new, like
        I've just been through the washing machine. Hung out

to dry more like. A bit s*tripey*. And that cow
    lick ain't fooling anyone love. I'd rather have been
        licked by an actual cow, the wetted dry, the warm fuzzy

meat, some bovine blessing. I ache at the back of my eyes
    Say: 'Yes! SO much better than before, thanks I really
        love it.' I hate it. Think about smoking a cigarette

thought that was over, it never occured to me
    while the milk poured from me but since getting
        untethered, it does cross my mind. Time to time, just:

One. Deep. Drag. Just to check my lungs still fill.
    Order a coffee in what I think is perfect Dutch, knocking
        that 'g' right out of its throaty park, the barista answers

in perfect English. I persist. He asks: 'Where are you from?'
    I answer: 'Ik heb mijn wortels in Engeland', which is to say:
        'I have my carrots in England'. Carrots? Roots I guess. But

I prefer carrots, *my* carrots, still there, blazing their
    patch of orange, home fires burning. It was always
        so close before, an arm and a leg away, now I think

of the black north sea and how much time we have.
    I waited so long to get my act together and now the
        theatre has gone dark. Think of wet autumn leaves on

       small muddy hands, old light flicking through summer drawn
           blinds. On my bike, the houses in the old Jordaan slant towards
               each other like trees reaching for the sun, the rain starts its

chatter on the water. We have a date. First
       in a year. Order a glass of champagne, talk
           about school days, hidden dreams and our

daughter's eczema cream. We watch the serving
       staff wafting the tables like clouds, watch the
           cleaning staff skirting the corridors like night,

I watch how you can always belong anywhere. Think of
       lines for a poem, sometimes on the days it hurts the most
           the more lines come. Wonder if it will always have a

grip on me, know I will never be the person who
       I long to be, who cartwheels off into the honeyed sunset
           shadow free. But does it matter if the breeze on my face

on my bike feels this glorious? The smell
       of the summer rain won't change or the
           yellow tulips like hamsa hands bobbing

       in ancient calm. Back home again.
           Google: best bedtime for a 17-month old.
               Google: can you dye over bad highlights.

Remember: there is a reason you fought your way to be
       here, fought your way to stay. Screaming into the black jaw
           of death for your life, and hers. 'Lucky you both made it',

they said. Lucky. Shudder it off. Google: top foods to boost fertility.
       Remember: your cells will renew and who you are now is dust.
           Blood then rust then dust. We have sex at three then too much tea

and it's my turn for pick up, I sweat in too many clothes in the
       humid May rain, coax quietness with raisins, think: in all honesty,
           I don't know what I'm doing. Find two curries in the freezer

       mix them together. Wait for the heat. Wonder if it's time to admit
           I might need god. Watch the sky. Turn my face towards the sunset
               where the embers rest, mirrored off the windows like the sky is on fire.

Lonely

You're lying close enough
that your eyes are black liquid stars
and I can count the constellations
of new sugar freckles on your skin
and taste your breath in mine.

And you tell me that you're lonely

not lonely alone, but something deeper
and more tangled that took you under,
and you wonder if it might soften
if you were surrounded by people
calling your name, or if you could

taste the salt of your mum's gyoza

again, or if your phone blinked back
more messages of assent, or if this
yawn of empty feeling could be stuffed
shut with stuff. You're close enough
that you can feel my heart beat back

and see in my eyes that I am lonely too

and roughly reflected there you see
that as sure as we have eyes to shine
and skin to freckle and breath to breathe
we will forever get lost in our loneliness
wandering tightly together, always alone

until we find where we know is home.

Last night we heard a shooting

Just before, my daughter stirred, perhaps she heard
the air go quiet in waiting, the silence sucked in
by two loud bangs: quick colon of cracks
and the washed moon watched, undisturbed.

The silence sucked in, the air went quiet,
the balcony opposite shone tiny blue screens
and undisturbed, the washed moon watched
a man embraced by yellow jackets, on the floor.

Blue screens shone from the balcony opposite
peering to capture the moment, already passed,
embraced by yellow jackets, a man on the floor.
We couldn't see if he was dead, or just resting.

The moment had passed, but still we peered,
they said he was disturbed, said there was a knife—
but was he dead, or just resting? We couldn't see.
Two boys in bouncy trainers walked past, laughing.

There was a knife, they said, he was crazy, they said,
there were two loud bangs: quick colon of cracks.
Two boys bounced past laughing, undisturbed.
Perhaps she heard, because my daughter stirred.

A walk in the park

On a perfect sunny Saturday
we take a walk in the park with our
brand new baby and the sky is the bluest
blue and the trees are the greenest green
and there is this glistening sheen and shine
to the day, a gentle breeze in the leaves, a rustle
of the reeds and the swans serene, slide by on the
navy water as the lily pads bobble and weave and

      I just want to *bite* you

walk two steps behind you
scouring for some resentment
of righteous reckoning, some new
transgression to bare teeth with, rip
flesh with, furious I have so little to play with
and you (confused) say *what's going on?* and I say *nothing*
(in that way we both know means it's definitely *something*)
so you ask me again, and I can't quite put my finger on it

      but I think it is maybe

because I am hot, hungry
because I am so fucking tired
because I can't do this anymore
because I can't not do this anymore
because my body is split open and spilling
guts, yes guts, and gore and blood and milk
because I almost died for this, would have died for this
because all *you* had to do was stick your penis in me, then

      wait for nine months

because I don't know who I am anymore
because I know I don't care who I was before
because my bones crack and cry because of this
because my heart flails bare because of this, ready for
impending catastrophe - and now this stupid joy is choking me
because I can't leave now, now love too much to leave, because I

felt the shadow pulse of another world come screaming through me
because I am standing on the edge of terrifyingly happy, and the fall

    will surely kill me.

But I don't say that, instead I hurl
something generic, far-reaching like
well, you never listen! and then start crying
so we stop on a bench and the tears fall
hot heavy plenty my face smeared with snot
and I mutter *sorry for being a dick*, and you (confused)
take my hand and say *hey, it's ok, it's a lot at the moment*
and I nod and we don't say anything for a while, we just

    sit and watch the trees.

Lullaby

awakening the ancient amphibian of sleep I split to wake
dreams dissolving like firework smoke, slow ghosts stray on

and I long to stay in their stories but I am already moving
ripped unzipped, splitting to wake, scuttling sleep-bleared

into your room, red rabbit night light and now lips on new skin
bundle-rocking hush-shushing you, like when we breathed as one

when we would hum holy through the day unthinking
you floating in the safe flesh shell we built between us

you traversing pilgrim arpeggios of deep blood breath
and now your life alive and in my arms and so I sing

your head flung back bow-arched in corkscrewed cry
jellied snot rattling lunged breath beating fevered time

so I will sing, repeat lul and bye until you fall back into it
your fingers curl-floating to sky as if in apparition found

as if in squally shadows a memory of your soaked divinity
angel of cells, blood-fastener, shape-shifter, I waited for you

soft-spettled spirit now in wild metal, mist of sleep-rubbed eyes
wet-edged they shine, so I will sing, blow breath on sweet sweat

until we are alone and not alone in the mouth of night
caught between worlds, so I will sing you to the other side

to the beyond but not beyond the beyond, you know that, right?
not that other beyond which jam-wakes me in the night

willing you to sleep but willing more to know you will wake
and when you wake I will sing-pray plea you back to sleep.

Your quavered breath slows tempo, white-blood calmed
so we wait for deeper waves to dip you into falling pools

white flowers come to meet you, tender shepherds near you
crystal chimes from chords of mine that split the middle night

I rock and you redeem, dropped back now to the other side
to the silver-close beyond, which will soon be burst by light.

Breathe

like now when
words come tumbling in and
arms get tightly tangled by
the hollow churn of night you
still recall that chink of light
that seeped through summer-drawn
blinds and the promises she made
to come back and check
you were asleep
but still alive
and earlier still
when shadows shifted
slowly through the indigo
crack between night and day
and you a small lit
silhouette bare feet on
threadbare carpet and her
waiting awake it seemed
her hands like cool china
calming the ragged heat
of middle night as you
crawl into the crack and
breathe
in and out with her
and earlier still when
you emerge breathless lifeless purple
leaving her unwillingly
with tightly tangled cord still
bound to blood and constant
breath and they pump you full
of air popping your tiny jelly fish
lung and sometimes now when
you feel you can't fill
those chambers full
with more than a clog of stale air
and words tumble lazily inwards
through all the wrong places
you think
if only she were here
breathing with you
breathing

When I wake to feed my daughter

Lockdown 2020

The light-filled days are simpler now
they shine in raging technicolour
life stripped bare to the bloom
        but was it always this bright?

and we watch stacked in our concrete
boxes, from our balconies and from
our newly washed windows
        and we watch it alone.

I march out my prayers along
pastel-chalked pavements
of hopscotch and hope
        swerve and smile at strangers

see blossom swirl, hear the hush
of the trees, watch white birds catch
the light of the shining sky
        old worries sent up in the sway

spend a moment to notice how the leaves
dance against my white kitchen wall
hear a wood-pigeon call, send love
        from the safety of my screen

but when I wake to feed my daughter

in the inky undulation of the night
I think about the certain wreckage
of it, the stubborn march of it, the
        too-soon tears of the bereaved

the mass graves and mask-marked faces
lungs watered in liquid, last breaths
no loved ones can witness
        and I wonder whether grief

will weave its way to my backdoor
as life as we know it sinks like a stone
can we rebuild in bricks and mortar
        or will it be blood and bone?

and I long for the open hills
at the back of my childhood home
and I long to show my mum the
        mother I have become

to lay my head in her lap and
feel her stroke my hair like she did
waiting again for her to say
        it will all be ok; *it will all be ok.*

Sometimes, who I am

Sometimes, I smoke one cigarette in the park, hiding behind
the Indian restaurant, listening to poems spoken in a soft Irish voice.

Sometimes, I wish those words were mine, watch daisies vibrate in the wind
write down the words 'feather' and 'crossable' and 'raven', just in case.

Sometimes, I silent-shout into my pillow at night pleading to the shining god
I half-remember just to send me back to sleep, just sleep – that's all.

Sometimes, I ride my bike fast into wind as trees lean into a tunnel –
a great green Mexican wave for my arrival, my heart fast and on fire

as the who I was then and the who I will be race to catch up with me.
What I would say to the who I was then is this: Tell the truth.

Tell the truth to that gleaming cluster of wanting you lugged around:
That the world will tilt and burn and smash your heart

But afterwards come feather cracks that leave room for light,
such light that clusters and rages in uncatchable pools.

Sometimes, the heron seems to know who I am, lone hunter
his blinking eye scorching forests for secret forage, knowing

sometimes I wish for a freedom that will never be mine
that once crossable river now a white wash of love and tethering

to raven hair and wild newness, soft-cell aliveness inching
with such light into the shadows that kept me safe for so long.

What I would say to the who I will be who races me through
the trees is this: the world tips, scorches, shatters, but anyway -

now it's too late to let go.

Light on the water

Under the blue gold sky
I watch you swim underwater
through the still and see-through sea
slicing shards of turquoise light.

You burst the surface to meet me
shaking silver drops in dancing arches
some sticking shining to your black hair
others trickling tiny rivers down your chest.

I see how the sea makes way for your body
as if it has been waiting for you to arrive:
golden water moulding to meet muscle
light shedding light onto your august skin.

I always thought you were of another world
but you fit so perfectly in this one
you, at home in the sea, your water
your sanshin sun sliding low to sleep.

I watch, wishing the sea would wash
the chewy air from my sticky skin
sand and oil and legs now coiled with yours
almost close enough to taste your ease.

Still now there are moments I watch you
submerge into your secret sea
every bone, breath, cell belonging
to where I long to go. But I can only go

back to when we bounced buoyant
skin touching skin touching water
untangling to stride up the sugarcane shores
stopping to take photos of our shadows in the sand.

(The sanshin is an Okinawan folk instrument similar to a banjo.)

Vespers

You seem tinier in the purple darkness than in daylight's bright tussle
where everything about you fills the space like rolling smoke.

Now, here, your hands stretch overhead in restful praise
shadow universes swirl behind new cells renewing and renewing

big ideas swell and settle around small bones
tiny lungs pump blood to growth and greatness

ears like smooth pearled seashells
waiting for the wave and the wash.

In this porcelain peace of night, you are still my baby -
away from the out-the-door, into-bed, behaving, stop-raging,

stop-wanting stop-asking be-faster kind of love, away from
the gentles and carefuls and pleases and thankyous

that I sculpt and smother you with, thinking that I know best.
But here baby, let it rage. Cross kingdoms of wonder and dark

that are only yours to find, ride the tides of sleep
into soft-grass dreams not the spikey, shouty ones

make chains from daisies thumbnailed into necklaces
spin stories together with the water and the music and the light.

Outside: the sun sinks the day to ground, the trees rustle lullabies.
Outside: the stars pump blood into their long moonlit fingers.

I pull the covers up to your chest, whisper 'goodnight, I love you'
now freed from all my waspy invitations and litany of no's

and I want to say: take it all, be it all, you are it all - but words won't do.
Outside: crocuses push through wet earth, ivy breaks brick

seeds float in the wind looking for a home, outside: the earth trembles
a concert for your wildness, which waits for you when you wake,

and the full night holds all the excesses of wonder that I cannot.
One breath invites another, you turn and murmur as I leave.

This morning, you made a butterfly on my bedroom wall with your hands:
ten tiny fingers that fluttered into focus before the creature grew

and blurred and vanished in an instant - a passing shadow painted
and absorbed by the brilliant morning sun.

A selection of things that have made it onto my long-term memory: Part 1

the milkman calling me 'little fatty' when I was three

and me, hiding from his broom-brush moustache in the
dark-angled gap behind the bobbled sofa

smashing dad's camera (sort of on purpose) on an airport floor
slamming my finger black in our yellow front door

sleepwalking summer nights, bare feet waking on threadbare carpet
honeysuckle wafting through open windows

Hail Marys said in assembly lines after lines until someone dropped
the easier prayer of sunned-tarmac school-holiday days

watching mum beat pulsed air into my brother's crackling lungs
eyes, bone-locked, black and soothing behind the mask

white-musked and bacardi-breezered, skirts rolled to raise eyebrows
and to find sticky redemption in the eyes of another

a piano teacher telling me to play Fantasia in D minor as if I had the flu
and later, waking with airwaves blocked to breathless pinhole

more antibiotics or antidepressants from the doctor, *something to fix*
the slow hued smudge of B&H on my fingertips

things falling, an iron lady, a black statue, a wall, a princess
killed on a hot August day and me, nearly new

and floating in a cold lake away from home
mountains printed the wrong way on the water

dropping daisy chains for thunderstorms, sprinting from a cracking sky
always wanting the light on, always asking for the light

being told *show off*, and later *too quiet*, being told I was *good*, until I wasn't
swallowing chewing gum and rage, though I knew I shouldn't

holding grannie's silk-bone hand as we crossed the road, her apricot
Max Factor powder lines, her head scarf neatly tied

and later, lighting a candle at her bedside the night she died.

Anything could happen

a therapist once told me anything could happen
which means *anything*

you could turn the corner and

meet your new true love or
trip and twist your ankle or

gulp a lung of honeysuckle
    reminding you of roller booting
    racktacktack down childish paths or

                                            you could catch
a virus skulking on the airstream
that hacks your life apart

or it could ride with you until it found
frailer hands to rest in

or a longed-for seed could choose to die
or choose to bloom in you

or a tumour could silently twist
into the bones of your beloved, or two cells
could conspire to save a

                                      life

    maybe yours
    or a war could weave its way to your backdoor
    and you'd wrap your babies warm in flesh on your

    basement floor
    or the sun could blind the driver's eyes
    as one of them runs
                    out into the road

    or a shadow could   pass the sun
                just in time

and you'd never know to say thank you to that cloud

    or you could watch your children watch the world burn
    releasing their hands to walk the blaze alone

    or simply watch them pick up the pain you've been carrying for years
    assuming it's theirs, *their* failings, *their* fears

    or you could smile at a stranger
    and save their day

                                                    but only today

and you could lie awake in the frayed edges
of navy-black night
counting regrets like year lines on a tree

sure that you can stay
a step ahead of it

       that a tighter grip on the stair rail
            will stop you
                    cracking to the floor

            that
cherry blossom will bloom harder still
    behind shut windows
    behind closed doors

    sure that cells
    will continue to gulp air and courage
flesh flawed and still forgiving

       sure that your children are sleeping
         soundly, and will do
            beyond you

    sure that the sky
    a new unadulterated blue
    could never have such violence

                     nor such grace
                     in store   only for you.

These Days

Lockdown 2020

Everyone I know keeps saying 'I can't wait for things to get back to normal!'
and I say, 'Oh yeah me too!'
but can I tell you a secret? I think I will miss

these days of quiet waiting
these days of slow walking, empty mornings
these days of all the *noticing*, like how

sunlight flickers like firelight behind morning-closed blinds
and how the swans bat their wings low over the black river
and how the blossom falls for fruit to bud and bloom

and oh, the trees! how they shine and breathe in layers of green on green

and how Venus surfaces against a dimming lilac sky
and how my lungs are full, and my legs are strong
and how I don't need fixing, after all

and how these days of repetition and repeat release
me from my slippery mythologies of success
so before I hurry back to normal, to the rushing fizz of it

let me stop to soak in the deep, clay quiet of these days
let me remember this holy boredom in my bones.

Post Traumatic Silence

I'm scared of silence   that kind at night
that kind that screws from spine to skull
that snaps eyes open to hoard dead light
that kind of silence where the world sleeps
oblivious to the chaos and catastrophe
that seeps unchecked inside of me
but then the noise gets me too   that kind of noise
that bashes my heart in breath-held fright
like a door slam bike backfire or lovers' fight
like a night-time scream   as if I might be ripping
from a dream   but only if I let myself sleep
safer to be on watch on vigil to the violence
of the heart pulsing jaw aching spine to skull silence
eyes open to keep in the light   that kind of light
the night tries to dim   but then again I'm scared
of silence that kind in the light that kind that tells me
to be still and to sit without flight   but don't they see
I need the busy to choke the chaos and catastrophe
that seeps unchecked inside of me so
I download an app to tell me to stop
or to remind me to mind my breath
or to remind me that death left
that I am here and still alive
and if I live who cares that I can't sit in silence
instead I can press play on some simulated raindrops
as the timer counts down for fifteen minutes
FIFTEEN   you must be joking I'll end up choking
on the memory of the blood cut scream suck
of the near miss didn't they say it was a near miss
but *you made it*   *she made it*   it was a near miss
but   *Yeah*   *We Made It*
so why doesn't it fade then   if the deer hunted
can shake it why can't I   I'll live haunted then
stay on red alert stop dead in my tracks ready for
chaos and catastrophe ready for this joy to start
choking me   ready to run from the silence that
kind at night run hard now run into the light
scared only of the still-lit embers of what I might
forget to remember   if only I could just breathe

into the eaves of it if only I could just face it
dead on head on I know I *know*
but I'm scared of silence that kind at night
that eyes open heart pulsing spine to skull silence
    so just give me the light
                              just give me the light

A butterfly landed in my palm

There is another meltdown, this time over nachos
something to do with sharing or having expected
mayonnaise or simply the general malaise of being
two and human. Later, we exchange cross words

as you fall asleep on the sofa, phone in hand,
and I say you could have emptied the dishwasher after
emptying it myself in that loudly silent way, slamming
drawers dropping pans stuttering the fuckerings so you'll

hear my righteous rage. Later, we go out to breathe the expanded
air, walk the way we always walk to the park. And then I see
a butterfly, a red and black butterfly, and I point to it, not
with my finger but with my palm upturned as if, let's say

in prayer. And the butterfly takes its cue and lands on
my palm, stays on my palm, and we all go quiet. Later,
I think about how I could Google *Red Admiral*, learn some intelligent
fact about how they feed on ivy flowers and maybe I could write

a poem about this *Vanessa Atalanta* (that's the one) that pulled me
out of my funk, taught me to appreciate the beauty of the moment,
the beauty of the little things. I could describe the underside of her wings
as the colour of a secret bruise, write something about marks of war woven

into a single pulse of peace, explain how my hands were strangely upturned
as if, say, in prayer, confess that she flew off in fleeting fanfare but not
before she changed my day around. But no: she stayed a beat too long. So
I shook my hand to thrust her off, disquieted by her vivid ease,

her capacity to stay. I shook her off, like how sometimes I close the
blinds as the sinking sun catches the edges of the clouds, like how
sometimes I turn from my new baby's new laugh, like
shaking off a butterfly. A casual backhand to the blaze.

Message from Earthside

If I could sit with you, you could tell me
that the light reflected on my skin was not from the sun
but from old stars, lines of constellations poured out from
some island galaxy mapped with my watery remembrance of light.

You were not set in stone, yet came anyway
set in cells   sweet blood   dark helix chains
answering the plea to make me new, not open to old orbits of abuse
they think I gave you life, but it's you who stitched mine back.

Afloat on the waves, your luminous spine shines
two halves of a brain beating from your silver spaceship
breathing in liquid   bouncing in moonlight   strung to an old heart
I think I met. Let me listen, tell me all
before you land   and we forget.

Fetching Isla

the hospital is just around the
corner, we can see it from our apartment
but the sat nav told you to take the back route

over speed bumps, round those tiny roundabouts
the new light on the dawn water shining broken crystals
that would have been beautiful. i curse you, repeatedly and we

arrive just in time for me to fall to all fours
feel hands and arms lead me to the water, water
not hot enough let it burn me if I am descending

water not deep enough let it drown me if this is the way i go.
i have been here before, preparing in the swollen days
for the descent, the transaction now fast approaching

limbs smashed against white porcelain
breath hollowed by unwinding howls
this: is where life goes to die

this: is where screams stop hearts
this: is where touching fingertips with death might
bring back a life, but i don't know whose

or if i'll be there too
this: is where it all went wrong before.
and so i leave you for a moment

my eyes lock yours then turn black and empty
my hips up bones floating in the bathtub, i left you
for a moment, your hands holding my

head in the water telling me it's done it's
done. It's Done. a parcel of slippery flesh handed
over and wet mushroom skin

skin sagging for stories to fill it and
hairy shoulders and nails already in need of a trim and
eyes searching for anything holy and unhuman.

this: is the agreement
a love too big to feel at once
and so i drink a coke, text my parents a photo '*here she is!*'

still vibrating still arriving still bound and pulsed together
feel her knowing mouth on my nipple
feel the blood pour out of me in rivers and rolling waves

wonder what just happened. search again for your eyes
resist the heavy hands of the midwife trying to ground me
i want to say: i'm trying to rise

                let   me   rise.

Second Marriage

This time we're walking, breath clear in the cold
the moon a sucked mint on washed morning skies
the trees on fire, bone willows burning gold
their flame reflected deep behind my eyes.

No fanfare this time, flowers or first dance
no favours, bridesmaids, or a puffed white dress
just us, just silence and a second chance
to offer each our glory and our mess.

The world goes on; just ours, this light, this breeze
seed promises take root, my hand in yours
just ours this shifting canopy of trees
where in my old green dress this time I'll roar

my Yes. To you, my second chance of grace
       this time I'll watch the sun light up your face.

If I was going to die tomorrow

If I was going to die tomorrow
I would leave the dishes in the sink and
dash to the dark lake, dive in headfirst
no time for toe dipping, feel the quench and
cooling rush of it, feel the coldness bite and
bathe my bones, splash my legs fast for the white
wash, shriek in glee for that girl I once knew.

I would leave the ruminations of early morning,
the sallow wallow of snooze, bounce up and watch
the birds in their morning busyness, greedily gulp the
air of one more day that life gets to live through me.
I would lie bare in the wet grass, ear to the ground
and listen for the deep cello creak of the earth, watch
a spider swirl out her silver thread on a blade of green.

I would wonder why I had waited so long
and call everyone I loved and say straight away
I love you and I'm sorry for all the mistakes
but shall we just dance now, dance out this mess?
and we would meet and eat and laugh and cry
and say: *but isn't this all wonderful, and
hasn't all this been wonderful?*

I would ask you to hold me tight at night
so no air could get between our bodies
welded now as one, and I would ask you to
name out loud all the things you loved, and
I would stay awake to listen to your sleeping
breath, steady as a heartbeat, deep as
the silence that always held me.

Things I nearly didn't notice on a day I felt depressed

the cool weight of the kitchen floor as it held me, then later

lying in bed where you put me, watching the way the dust

caught the light

particles suspended, white planets

pulled slowly towards the sun

your face close to mine, holding hands by our mouths and you

kissing my knuckles and saying things, I know you

said nice things

you scribbling a shopping list on an old envelope

at the kitchen table, our daughter on your lap

the feeling of the bonfire in the park on my face

the oily distortion of dogs and happiness

behind the glow

our daughter's red-cold pudgy hands patting down sand

in her bucket, her chasing pigeons from their pecking

the way the wings

of a seagull were backlit by the sinking sun on the rooftop

golden bones stretching

up to sky.

Watching Dumbo in Yokohama

This time, the cuckoo clock still cuckoos
once on the half hour too

you have to be quick to catch him, I tell you.

mosquito smoke coils up heavy
in the humid September heat, cicadas chirp behind
white tin blinds, we drink cold barley tea from old
Peter Rabbit cups, eat white toast, thick cut
with cherry jam, wait for the next cuckoo
call to mark the empty day

Here we are, in your land of shimmering shrines
last time, the seed of a thought by the light on the water
this time, more life than any thought can hold

face shining and asking
hair black and sticking to your hot forehead
eyes like dark lit marbles
hands still chubby and looking to feel
the world into fast understanding.

Here you are, lying easy on the tatami floor
here you are, looking like the people in the photos on the wall
typhoons brew and pass
wet storms horizontal and expected

walls that keep us confined and alive and aware of
our human itch to run and numb, and this we share.

I know, this moment will pass
I know, I will look back and remember
Baba putting on Dumbo again as we sit sticking together
you, following the story in dubbed Japanese
your hot shoulder burrowing into my hot side

and I'm hot and humid and bitten and impatient and
I'm looking for an escape
from this nowness, from your needs.

I know, your needs will soon leave my side
and I will fold your summer clothes to put away
and pass on next year
when a new you will be here.

This moment I long to leave will soon be
the one I long to relive, in all its golden

weight, waiting for the cuckoo to call
watching Dumbo in Yokohama
your hot shoulder burrowing into my hot side.

And what about the prayers?

1.

Sometimes I think of the prayers that were said for me
worry worked out from beads of caress-smoothed cedar
psalms and supplications said on my confirmation day
even though I felt like a fraud for my hot and itchy heart
prayers for blessing and safe passage and health and oh –
nothing specific, just divine protection (you know the stuff)
and later the prayers of middle-night, sleepless petitions to
get me out of a marriage or unwind from addictions, those
dark velvet tongue-fuzzing wild and winding prayers that
later crossed oceans to find Siddhartha and shining Shinto
shrines (spirits always watching) and new prayers for safe
delivery, for life on life, those answered and em-bodied prayers
later sticking stubby toddler hands in the ancestor incense ash
before I can reach them: a quick lick of holy in their hot and
                                        prayerless world.

2.

When I introduced my three-year-old to the felty Baby Jesus
in the nativity scene, she grabbed him and said:
        'Come with me Babyccinno, I'll take care of you'

and I wondered whether we should get busy finding
her some blessed bodyguards other than this god of
Milk and Froth she was fist-clenching the life out of

but not knowing where to begin, with all the:

sacred screens and see-to-believes
and meditations-for-one, of micro-dosing and
pendulum-dousing of ice breathing and crystals
bathing in moonlight for protection, from mercury
retrograding the shit out of everything   – *again!*

Then again, aren't we lucky that we don't have to sit
in wooden pews and smell flagstone damp and coffee-breath
on hymns and listen to the lists of our wrongs and wranglings

rather – we can declare hand on heart:
>   *'You know, I'd say I'm not religious, I'm spiritual'*

And be greeted by an interested nod, or:
>   *'The universe has my back!'*

(Jesus, whatever you do, don't mention God)

But will they feel lost, my daughters, without
>   that Big Man in the sky or
>   that Smaller Man under the tree
>   (hey, it's not me, we grew up with the He's)

>   and what about the prayers?

3.

I guess I could say: I carry them in my heart all day.
It might be a cliché, but to lug another two hearts around as
well as your own verges on the Biblical. I guess I could say

I micro-dose prayers to them at night, my hand stroking
hot foreheads, my song hidden inside the song
My Bonnie Lies Over the Ocean: Oh God, So Much Could Go Wrong

I guess the worry woven into my old bones is my
breast-beating, begging he/him/she/her/they/theirs
to protect them from It All. I could say that I hunger

for the holy, or for redemption lying in the morning grass
or for confession in my fading flesh, I guess in this
earth-deep itch sprinting through my cells something

must start to stick? I guess I can show them how the sky
and the trees can shake the shame from their skin, how the
light shining behind their eyes is the place to begin, I guess

what I'm saying is:

>   could (you) protect them without my prayers?
>   nothing to unmake them, no end that's an end
>   if this counts? if (you) hear me? if (you're) there?

>   (Amen)

Note-to-self

I don't want to look back
        and realise this whole time I was

happy, when my daughters leave home to get their hearts
        broken, and the empty mornings and tidy rooms yawn

wide in scrubbed peacefulness, I don't want
        to look back and realise that I miss being

needed, that I miss being tired, that sometimes
        I even miss scraping scrambled eggs off table legs

that I miss the heavy head heavy breath
        dark fuzz of hair silk skin tucked under my

cheek, that I miss being adored for who
        I am, before they find out who I really am

centred at the centre of their tiny universe
        their sea-black eyes orbiting mine.

There are many ways to view a body

'Oh NO mummy, they fell down!'
said my three-year-old in the bath
pointing at my nipples, all stretched and
slumped like two tiny chipolatas, pink pellets
sagging slowly onto my small boobs like empty
zip-lock bags after the picnic is over. On a good day
I think, they did good! - these once-swollen power houses
pumping nectar to my babies, my glorious womanhood
oozing just, everywhere, all milk and flesh and life
brimmed to breaking point, all luscious, lascivious
and pouring forth. On other days I hide them
hurriedly, these sad sacks hung out to dry,
wonder about those perky Insta-boobs,
all caramel skinned and tightly
cradled in tangerine bikini triangles,
flesh bursting with invitation (perky, but
not porn, promise) and wonder if that's really
what my husband would like. He says he likes my sweet
little once-udders, still touched-out, still hidden under a bra
during sex, my one-year-old still sometimes lunging at them
laughing, teeth-bared, my three-year-old still sometimes flicking
their falling heads in the bath. But they grew my babies, these
baps, these boobs, these breasts grew my babies with these
wonky woman hips, this prolapsed pelvic floor, these
sags of skin rolling over a collapsed core, these
stretch marks, these pounds I can't shift, this
blood I still shed, this tender back, these
battered bones, these nipples that fell.

This whole body. This holy, holy body.

Birds

The branches above are breaking into the sky —
as birds like ink on air swirl from trees to flight
great black lungfuls of them freewheeling across
the white winter sky, humming the secret rhythm
of fragment to solid, then loosening into dance.
Look up.

I wonder what it is in me that still fears my light
turning instead to the sharp inhale of darkness —
and I keep thinking: don't let me mess this up
me, with my gaze skewed down to tangled ground
missing this quiet kindness, this wild mess, this show.
Be still.

The sky is still mine if I want it
the ground doesn't care if I'm a poet or a mother
the birds don't care if the words fly out of me
or fester on vein branches in my mind
waiting for the perfect moment to be set free.
Let go.

Fear comes when you have something to lose.
Once, I was a puffin on a cliff-face, a hedgehog in a thicket,
a terrapin watching shadows blur on faces in the morning sun.
Once, I was the white on the wave and the notes on a piano
playing until the dark in my heart became a song taking flight.

Under the light of a single star, I waited blindly
for the call, for the hair-breath moment of arriving
looking at the light for the first time shining —
and a mother not sure if her child had survived.
Once, I squeezed through a star-hole to be here,

once, I hopscotched across the dark glass sky
to claim my name, once I was the wind and the light
riding hidden eddies to a freedom I didn't know was mine.
Once, I counted tears until they became stars in the sky —
or poems: blossoming, or birds: laughing.
Take flight.

A selection of things that have made it onto my long-term memory: Part 3

clocking your light

and you: telling me about a barbeque you had been to at the weekend

and me: wondering what it would be like to spend a day with you

our first argument a few days after you moved in, over a box of books

but really it was because we were both scared for our beaten-up hearts

the light reflected on the water the day we said we'd try for a baby

and later, driving down sugarcane corridors hunting for stars

for handfuls of light, just ours

circling cobbled canals the wind on my face my second chance at grace

smoking a rollie on the balcony while a curry cooked on the stove

before realising I should do a pregnancy test, and later

my waters being broken with what looked like a magic wand

and this thought: one of us at the very least will die here, somehow

reaching for grannie's silk-bone hand again, breathe, they

said, breathe, they said, and later

releasing the final scream to that wall of death, and later:

      holding that first wild aliveness.

Dream

I had a dream the world was ending
it sounds too big for a dream
but there it was

just you and me driving into the eye of it
against a twilit sky, gold popcorn clouds
wondering who would

help us if we were all left to perish
but not minding too much, hearing the
lazy lilt of bells

chime a familiar melody, just you and me
knowing the world in its strange beauty
would still gleam

after we were gone. And when I woke
I thought of the gold popcorn clouds
and wanted to know

how it ended, tried to go back to the dream
back to the tilted, gilded sorrow,
back to that last

deep surrender, hoping to catch the
final answer to *what is it that we are
here to remember?*

*

Acknowledgements

'**These Days**': Published by Acumen Poetry, Volume 98

'**Day Off**': Published by Prairie Fire, Volume 43

'**Lullaby**': Published by The Rappahannock Review, Issue 8.2

'**And what about the Prayers**': Published by The Dewdrop, February 2024

'**Lonely**': Selected as a winner of Arvon's 5-day poetry competition, 2019

'**There are many ways to view a body**': Shortlisted for the Creative Ink Poetry Prize 2023 and published by Tangled Locks Journal, May 2024

'**Fetching Isla**', '**If I was going to die tomorrow**' and '**Watching Dumbo in Yokohama**': Published by Eunoia Review, May 2024

'**When I wake to feed my daughter**': Published by Posh Dog Press in their 'Lockdown Anthology'

'**Sometimes who I am**': Published by Beyond Words Literary Journal, Volume 54, January 2025

Originally from Oxford (UK) Jo Matthews is a freelance writer and copywriter living in Amsterdam, the Netherlands. Her poetry and writings have appeared in Popshot magazine, Acumen, Prairie Fire, The Rappahannock Review, Literary Mama and Tangled Locks Journal - among others. She was recently short-listed for the Creative Ink Poetry Prize and is currently studying for an MSc in Creative Writing for Therapeutic Purposes. She is a proud mum to two young daughters (who are both keeping her young and ageing her rapidly). You can find out more about Jo at www.jo-matthews.com.

Also Available from Cathexis Northwest Press:

Something To Cry About
by Robert Krantz

Suburban Hermeneutics
by Ian Cappelli

God's Love Is Very Busy
by David Seung

that one time we were almost people
by Christian Czaniecki

Fever Dream/Take Heart
by Valyntina Grenier

The Book of Night & Waking
by Clif Mason

Dead Birds of New Zealand
by Christian Czaniecki

The Weathering of Igneous Rockforms in High-Altitude Riparian Environments
by John Belk

If A Fish
by George Burns

How to Draw a Blank
by Collin Van Son

En Route
by Jesse Wolfe

sky bright psalms
by Temple Cone

Moonbird
by Henry G. Stanton

southern athiest. oh, honey
by d. e. fulford

Bruises, Birthmarks & Other Calamities
by Nadine Klassen

Wanted: Comedy, Addicts
by AR Dugan

They Curve Like Snakes
by David Alexander McFarland

the catalog of daily fears
by Beth Dufford

Shops Close Too Early
by Josh Feit

Vanity Unfair and Other Poems
by Robert Eugene Rubino

Destructive Heresies
by Milo E. Gorgevska

Bodies of Separation
by Chim Sher Ting

The Night with James Dean and Other Prose Poems
by Allison A. deFreese

About Time
by Julie Benesh

Suspended
by Ellen White Rook

The Unempty Spaces Between
by Louis Efron

Quomodo probatur in conflatorio
by Nick Roberts

Suspended
by Ellen White Rook

Call Me Not Ishmael but the Sea
by J. Martin Daughtry

Wild Evolution
by Naomi Leimsider

Coming To Terms
by Peter Sagnella

Acta
by Patrick Wilcox

Honeymoon Shoes
by Valyntina Grenier

Practising Ascending
by Nadine Hitchiner

Home Visit
by Michal Rubin

LA CIUDAD EN TI: THE CITY WITHIN YOU
by Karla Marrufo
Translated from the Spanish by Allison A. deFreese

Resin in the Milky Way
by Amanda Rabaduex

Bone Hunting
by Trinity Catlin

Muskets for the Bear Problem
by Andrew Whitmer

Self-Portraits as a Reddening Sky
by Samuel Gilpin

Desert
by Eric Larsh

Leaving the Religion of Self-Harm
by Bailey Blumenstock

Fractured Symphony
by Andi Myles

La dulzura de los naufragios: The Sweetness of Shipwrecks
by Karla Marrufo
Translated from the Spanish by Allison A. deFreese

Love & Fear
by Henry G. Stanton

The Longed For Longer For
by Sibani Sen

Brood
by Kelly Granito

Bleeding Ghosts
by Lara Chamoun

As Jaguars Dreamed On The Earth's Dark Face
by Clif Mason

Cathexis Northwest Press

www.ingramcontent.com/pod-product-compliance
Lightning Source LLC
Chambersburg PA
CBHW020443090526
44586CB00045B/812